Tilak had a wobbly tooth.

He showed it to the postman.

He showed it to Rosie.

He went into the shop

and he showed it to Mo.

'Oh, no!' said Tilak.

His wobbly tooth had gone.

Everybody looked for Tilak's tooth.

They looked in boxes.
They looked on the floor.

They looked under the table and
behind the door.

Tilak's tooth had gone.

Mum gave him a hug.

Dot gave him a biscuit.

PULL

The biscuit had two eyes,
a nose, a mouth and . . .

Tilak's tooth!